REDEFINING FINANCIAL WELL-BEING:

A Holistic Approach to Wealth and Happiness

GINA . H. HARRISON

Redefining financial well-being

Table of contents

Chapter one

<u>Recognizing financial health</u>

The entire condition of a person's or a household's financial stability and health is referred to as financial well-being. It includes more than just having money; it also includes things like being able to handle stress, achieve financial goals, and make wise financial judgments. Effective budgeting, saving, investing, and debt management are all necessary to achieve financial well-being while keeping one's values and financial objectives in mind. A sense of financial freedom and tranquility is the goal of this all-encompassing approach to financial health. It involves a number of dimensions, such as:

1. **Financial security** is the state of having an emergency fund and insurance, as well as a steady and reliable source of income to meet one's fundamental necessities and unforeseen expenses.

2. **Financial freedom** is the capacity to manage your finances without feeling bound by them. This may involve saving, investing, and spending on the things that are most important to you.

3. **Debt management** is the process of efficiently controlling and lowering debt

while averting disproportionate debt loads that may put a strain on finances.

4. **Spending and creating a budget** are crucial components of successful money management and reaching your financial objectives. To establish a plan for prudent money allocation, you must evaluate your income, expenses, and financial objectives while creating a budget.

5. **Investments and Savings**: To increase wealth over time, set aside a portion of your salary on a regular basis and make wise investment decisions.

6. **Financial Literacy and Knowledge**: Possessing the knowledge and abilities needed to make wise financial decisions, including an awareness of issues like taxes, investment possibilities, and interest rates.

7. **Financial Goals and Planning**: Whether you're saving for retirement, purchasing a home, or paying for school, you need to set specific financial goals and create a strategy to reach them.

8. **Financial Health in Partnerships**: preserving harmonious financial habits and communication within families or relationships in order to prevent disputes and advance common financial objectives.

9.**Financial Resilience**: Having plans in place to overcome financial obstacles and being ready for unforeseen financial losses.

10. **Emotional Well-Being**: Understanding the link between financial strain and psychological well-being, and proactively attempting to lessen financial stressors.

The Significance of having Sound Financial Standing

For both people and families, financial well-being is essential since it has a direct impact on many areas of their lives. The following examples demonstrate why having sound financial standing is crucial:

1. **Taking Care of Basic Needs**: A person's ability to pay for necessities like food, shelter, healthcare, and education is a sign of their financial well-being. It gives them a feeling of stability and security in their lives.

2. **Lessened tension**: Being able to pay for essentials and maintain control over one's finances reduces tension. Thus, a healthier lifestyle in general is encouraged and mental and emotional well-being is enhanced.

3. **Achieving goals and Objectives**: Possessing financial stability enables people to establish and meet their financial objectives. The pursuit of personal goals is made possible by financial security, whether those goals are saving for a down payment on a home, making retirement plans, or going back to school.

4. **Emergency Preparedness**: Unexpected events, like medical crises, job losses, and natural disasters, are a part of everyday life. People who are in a comfortable financial position can deal with these kinds of circumstances without going into serious debt or risking their long-term savings.

5. **Freedom and Independence**: By lowering dependency on outside sources of income, financial stability fosters freedom and independence. Rather than being constrained by budgetary limitations, it gives people more freedom to make decisions that are consistent with their values and goals.

6. **Better Relationships**: Relationship tension and conflict are sometimes caused by financial strain. Financial stability, on the other hand, promotes healthier relationships by reducing financial conflicts and freeing up couples and families to concentrate on strengthening their bonds.

7. **Long-Term Financial Security**: Long-term financial security is based on the development and maintenance of financial well-being. It includes actions like investing, saving, and retirement planning, which enable people to continue living the way they want to long after they leave the workforce.

The Traditional as well as Contemporary Perspectives on Financial Security

A key component of a person's total life pleasure is their financial well-being. Saving money, living within one's means, and avoiding needless debt are frequently highlighted in traditional perspectives on financial well-being. This viewpoint highlights how crucial it is to save money for emergencies, prepare for retirement, and practice frugal spending.

However, contemporary perspectives on financial well-being adopt a more comprehensive stance. There is a greater focus on coordinating financial decisions with long-term objectives and personal beliefs, even though saving and avoiding debt are still advised. This viewpoint acknowledges that financial well-being includes emotional fulfillment and well-being in addition to simply acquiring riches. Current strategies for financial well-being encourage people to make budgets that allow for discretionary spending on items that fulfill and offer them delight in addition to covering necessities. This change in perspective recognizes that money shouldn't be a cause of stress or deprivation, but rather a tool for improving one's quality of life.

Additionally, modern views on financial well-being recognize the importance of informed spending decisions. This means being mindful of purchases, considering the long-term value and impact of each expenditure, and evaluating whether the item or experience aligns with personal values and goals. It involves questioning the societal pressures of consumerism and making conscious choices that bring genuine satisfaction and fulfillment.

The Elements of Well-Being Aside from Money

The various aspects of well-being mental, physical, social, and emotional are interrelated and have a substantial influence on one's financial well-being. Let's examine the relationship between these elements and financial well-being:

1. **Mental Health**: A person's psychological state, encompassing their thoughts, feelings, and general mental

health, is referred to as their mental well-being. Because mental health has an impact on risk-taking tendencies, decision-making skills, and the capacity to successfully plan and manage resources, it can also have an impact on financial well-being. For instance, those who are under a lot of stress or anxiety could be more likely to spend impulsively or make bad financial decisions.

2. **Physical Well-Being**: A person's physical health and vitality are all part of their physical well-being. Being in good physical condition helps lower insurance and medical costs, which can improve financial stability.

3. **Social Well-Being**: A person's sense of belonging, social support, and relationship quality are all indicators of their social well-being. Having strong social links can help one's financial situation because they can be a source of support, networking, and collaboration when things go tough. Furthermore, a strong social network can give access to data regarding financial resources, job openings, and financial literacy.

4. **Emotional Well-Being**: The capacity to successfully handle and regulate one's emotions is a key component of emotional well-being. Through influencing spending patterns and financial decision-making,

emotional well-being can have an impact on financial well-being. For example, it could be difficult for someone who struggles with impulse control or emotional spending to keep to a budget or make wise financial decisions.

In general, there are both direct and indirect interactions between these aspects of well-being and financial well-being.It is vital to tackle all facets comprehensively in order to attain a sound financial existence. Financial decision-making, budgeting abilities, and general financial stability can all be positively impacted by taking care of one's mental, physical, social, and emotional well-being.

Consequently, adopting behaviors that advance well-being in each of these domains can have a big impact on one's financial status and long-term financial objectives.

Chapter two

<u>Financial Education and Literacy</u>

Essential elements of individual financial well-being are financial education and literacy. They entail gaining the information and abilities necessary to manage finances, create budgets, save money, invest, and comprehend financial services and goods.People who are financially literate can build a strong basis for wise financial decisions. It enables people to comprehend essential financial ideas that are necessary to make wise financial decisions regarding their own finances, including as interest rates, inflation, and compound interest.By giving people the information and resources they need to successfully navigate the complicated world of personal finance, financial education programs and materials aim to increase financial literacy. These programs can be offered in a variety of formats, such as community projects, online classes, workshops, and advice from financial experts.People who possess greater financial literacy are better equipped to handle their finances. They can increase their financial stability and long-term financial well-being by making wiser decisions regarding their spending, saving, and investing. Avoiding financial traps like debt, fraud, and exploitative lending practices also heavily depends on having a solid financial literacy.

Furthermore, vulnerable groups—such as young adults, those with low incomes, and those who might not have easy access to financial resources—should pay particular attention to financial literacy. We can support financial inclusion and aid in closing the wealth and opportunity gap by educating these populations about money matters.

The Significance Of Financial Knowledge

It is impossible to exaggerate the value of financial literacy. It is a vital ability that enables people to comprehend and decide on their personal money with knowledge. People that are financially literate are better able to plan for the future, create objectives, and manage their money.Making wise financial decisions is made possible by having a solid foundation in financial literacy. It aids in their understanding of ideas like debt management, investing, saving, and budgeting.Armed with this information, people may watch their spending, set realistic budgets, and decide what to spend and save.

Additionally, financial literacy gives people the ability to successfully negotiate the complicated financial world. It makes financial products and services like credit cards, loans, mortgages, and insurance easier for people to understand. People can compare possibilities, locate the greatest offers, and steer clear of financial traps with the use of this expertise.

Furthermore, resilience and financial security are directly correlated with financial literacy. It aids people in defending themselves against financial scams and fraud. It also offers the resources required to build retirement, emergency, and unforeseen spending plans.Young adults need financial literacy even more as they become more independent and take charge of their financial lives. They can acquire sound financial habits and make wise decisions right away if they are given early financial education and skills. Financial literacy is essential to one's own financial security. It gives people the ability to comprehend money and make wise financial decisions. People can increase their financial security, make future plans, and reach their financial objectives by developing their financial knowledge and skills.

Basic financial ideas that everyone should understand

To better comprehend their own finances and make wise decisions, everyone should be aware of a few basic financial concepts. These consist of:

1. **Budgeting**: Budgeting entails making a plan for how to divide your money between your goals for savings and expenses. It assists you in keeping tabs on your expenditures, setting financial priorities, and preventing overspending.

2. **Saving**: Saving is the process of reserving a part of your earnings for later usage. Saving money is crucial for unexpected costs, large purchases, and long-term objectives like retirement. It contributes to achieving financial stability and acts as a safety net during hard times.

3. **Debt Management**: This entails identifying the many forms of debt, including mortgages, student loans, and credit card debt, as well as creating plans to appropriately manage and pay off debt. This entails avoiding excessive debt, lowering interest expenses, and making on-time payments.

4. **Investing**: Investing is the process of placing your money with the intention of earning returns over time in assets like stocks, bonds, or real estate. To make wise investment choices, it's critical to comprehend fundamental ideas, risks, and diversification.

5. **Interest Rates**: The cost of borrowing money or the yield on investments is represented by interest rates. Understanding interest rates is essential because they affect savings growth, investment returns, and borrowing costs.

6. **Credit Score**: Your creditworthiness is represented numerically by your credit score. It has an impact on your capacity to obtain financial goods, obtain favorable interest rates, and borrow money. Financial well-being depends on knowing how credit ratings are determined and how to keep a high credit score.

7. **Insurance**: Insurance serves as a safeguard against monetary losses brought on by unforeseen circumstances like illness, accidents, or property damage. Making educated decisions about safeguarding your possessions and self requires having a thorough understanding

of the many insurance kinds, their costs, and their coverage.

Planning Your Finances And Budget

To successfully manage your finances and reach your financial objectives, financial planning and budgeting are crucial tools. Below is an explanation of these ideas:

1. **Budgeting**: A budget is a financial plan, usually monthly, that shows your revenue and outlays for a given period of time. It aids in prudent financial management and expenditure tracking. To make a budget, do the following:

- **Determine your income**: Calculate your monthly gross income from all sources.

- **Enumerate your spending**: Put all of your monthly costs down on paper, including variable costs like groceries, entertainment, and travel, as well as fixed costs like electricity, insurance, and rent or a mortgage.

- **Set monetary objectives**: Set both short- and long-term objectives, such as funding a trip, paying off debt, or putting money aside for emergencies.

- **Distribute your earnings**: Set aside a portion of your money for savings and expenses. Make sure your spending doesn't go beyond your earnings.

- **Monitor and adapt**: To stay inside your budget, evaluate your spending on a regular basis and make modifications as necessary.

2. **Financial Planning**: This entails drawing out a plan for your future finances. To accomplish those objectives, it entails establishing objectives, formulating plans of action, and making defensible choices. Here are a few crucial financial planning components:

- **Emergency fund**: Put money away for unforeseen costs such as lost wages or medical expenditures in an emergency fund. Three to six months' worth of living expenditures should be your goal.

- **Debt management**: Make a strategy to control and eventually pay off whatever debt you may have, including student loans and credit card debt.

- **Savings and investing**: To gradually accumulate wealth, make regular savings and investments. Take into account several investing possibilities, depending on your financial goals and risk tolerance, such as stocks, bonds, mutual funds, or real estate.

- **Retirement planning**: Set aside money for retirement by funding individual retirement accounts (IRAs) or 401(k)s. To determine how much you'll need for a decent retirement, use retirement calculators.

- **Insurance coverage**: To safeguard your finances and the financial security of your loved ones, evaluate your insurance needs, including health, life, and property insurance.

- **Estate planning**: To make sure your intentions are carried out in the future, think about drafting a will, designating beneficiaries, and setting up a power of attorney and health care directives.

As your circumstances change, examine and update your financial strategy and budget on a regular basis. If required, get guidance from financial experts. You may make wise financial decisions and work toward a more secure financial future by engaging in budgeting and financial planning activities.

<u>Earning And Professional Development</u>

There are various tactics you can think about in order to optimize your income potential:

1. **Improve your education and abilities**: Take classes, attend workshops, or enroll in post secondary education programs to consistently expand your knowledge and abilities. This may increase your value and marketability in your industry, which may open doors to better employment or allow you to charge more for your services as a consultant or freelancer.

2. **Take into account prospects for career advancement**: Seek methods to advance in your present work or investigate different fields where more profitable jobs might be accessible. Finding and seizing these kinds of chances can be facilitated by networking and forming connections with experts in your industry.

3. **Increase the size of your professional network** : Participate in online forums, attend business events, and join organizations for professionals. Developing a strong network can open up new options for collaboration, referrals,

and access to resources that can raise your earning potential.

4. **Determine your market value**: To be sure you are getting paid appropriately, find out what the going rates or average pay in your field are. If you discover that your pay is below what the industry average is, think about bargaining for a raise or looking into other career paths.

5. **Diversify your sources of revenue**: Find strategies to bring in a variety of sources of money. This may be creating a side business, investing in stocks or real estate, or taking on freelancing or

consulting work in addition to your day job. By spreading out your income, you can potentially boost your total profits while reducing the risk of depending only on one source.

Recall that it may require patience, persistence, and time to maximize your earning potential. Setting specific targets and regularly reviewing and adjusting your tactics are crucial as you move closer to your financial goals.

Advancement and Career Development

When optimizing your earning potential, career development and progress are crucial considerations. The following tactics will assist you in this regard:

1. **Make specific career goals**: Establish your long-term professional goals and the steps necessary to reach them. This will provide you a distinct feeling of purpose and empower you to choose wisely from the chances that present themselves.

2. **Always learn new things and up skill**: Adopt a growth mentality and make an effort to expand your knowledge and skill set. Utilize professional development options to expand your knowledge and keep current with industry trends. Examples of these opportunities include

webinars, workshops, seminars, and online courses.

3. **Actively seek mentorship and feedback**: To pinpoint areas for development and progress, ask mentors, colleagues, or supervisors for their opinions.Their knowledge and perceptions might be quite helpful to you as you progress in your profession.

4. **Network strategically**: Participate at industry events, affiliate with associations that are pertinent to your field, and establish and preserve a robust professional network. Numerous chances,

such as joint ventures, employment opportunities, and access to priceless resources, might arise through networking.

5. **Accept difficult assignments**: Offer your assistance with tasks or projects that force you to step outside of your comfort zone and give you the chance to learn new abilities or become familiar with various facets of your industry. This shows that you're willing to take on challenges and may make you stand out when prospects for job progression present themselves.

6. **Build great leadership and communication skills**: In the business, the

ability to lead and communicate effectively is highly regarded. By looking for chances to oversee projects, working with varied teams, and improving your communication and persuasion skills, you can work on building these abilities.

7. **Keep up with industry trends**: Keep abreast of the most recent advancements and new trends in your field. Being up to date on developments in the industry can help you stay ahead of the curve in terms of professional progression prospects and add significant value to your firm. Keep in mind that promotion and career development are not instantaneous. It's an ongoing process that calls for persistence,

forbearance, and initiative. To support your professional development and raise your earning potential, regularly assess your progress, ask for feedback, and make necessary adjustments to your methods.

Passive Sources Of Income

A great method to augment your income and raise your potential revenue is through passive income streams. Consider the following typical passive income suggestions:

1. **Rental properties**: Real estate investments have the potential to produce a steady stream of passive income through rental payments. Both hiring a property

manager and making your own investments in residential or commercial properties are options.

2. **Dividend-paying stocks**: Investing in dividend-paying businesses might result in passive income. A company will distribute a portion of its profits as dividends to its owners. Examine and choose stocks with a history of consistent dividend payments and possibilities for expansion.

3. **Peer-to-peer lending**: Websites exist where individuals can lend money to one another and receive interest. By methodically reinvested interest,

peer-to-peer lending can help you create passive income.

4. **Create and market digital items**: Digital goods such as e-books, online courses, templates, and graphics can be created and sold repeatedly. Digital products can be sold on platforms such as Amazon Kindle Direct Publishing and Udemy.

5. **Affiliate marketing**: You can profit from affiliate marketing by promoting the products and services of others. You can utilize email marketing, social media accounts, or your own blog for this. When

someone makes a purchase using your referral link, you get paid a commission.

6. **Intellectual property royalties**: You can be eligible to get royalties as a passive source of income if you are the author of books, songs, or patents. By licensing it, you can allow third parties to utilize your intellectual property in return for income.

7. **Create a software or mobile app**: Although developing a software or mobile app can take some time, once it's out there, user downloads, in-app purchases, and subscriptions can generate passive income.

Keep in mind that setting up passive income streams typically requires upfront costs and labor. Thorough consideration and preparation are necessary to find a passive income plan that complements your interests, skills, and financial goals.

Balancing work with Health Maintaining

A balance between work and well-being is necessary to maintain overall health and happiness. The following strategies will help you achieve a more advantageous balance:

1. **Set boundaries**: Make clear distinctions between your personal and work lives.

Clearly define your working hours and try not to exceed them by not working overtime. To let people know when you're available, make sure your clients and colleagues are aware of your boundaries.

2. **Give yourself enough attention**: Make time for activities that improve your physical, mental, and emotional well-being. Get enough sleep, maintain a good diet, work out frequently, and engage in enjoyable pursuits like hobbies or spending time with close friends and family. Taking care of yourself will allow you to rejuvenate and perform better in all areas of your life.

3. **Use time management techniques** to increase productivity and efficiency during business hours. Prioritize your tasks, delegate tasks to others when you can, and avoid multitasking since it may reduce your focus and productivity. Setting realistic deadlines and breaking up challenging tasks into smaller, more manageable segments are other ways to reduce stress.

4. **Employ constructive stress-reduction techniques**: To help you manage your stress, try mindfulness training, deep breathing techniques, or calming activities like yoga or meditation. Regularly pausing

during the day to relax and refuel can help greatly lower your stress levels.

5. Interact with your clients and employer: If you're struggling to achieve balance or feel overworked, be honest and transparent with your boss and clients. To reach a solution that works for you both, discuss your concerns, investigate potential solutions, and work together.

6. **Foster a pleasant work environment**: Encourage a positive work environment where people are encouraged to prioritize their health. Encourage and respect the boundaries that your colleagues have set, and collaborate to find flexible solutions that allow everyone to maintain a healthy

work-life balance. Maintaining a healthy work-life balance requires ongoing adjustments when circumstances spiral out of control. To create a better balance that will allow you to thrive on both a personal and professional level, make the necessary modifications and routine reviews.

Chapter three

<u>The psychology of money</u>

Examining the relationship between people and their financial decisions is the subject of the intriguing field of money psychology. It explores the different facets that impact our views, convictions, and actions around money.The idea of financial psychology is one facet of the psychology of money; it enables us to comprehend how our financial behaviors are shaped by our money mindset. The way we view money can be greatly influenced by our cultural background, prior experiences, and upbringing.Some people may view money as a source of stability and security, which makes them cautious and risk-averse with their finances. To some, accumulating wealth and material belongings are more important than anything else because they see money as a sign of power or success.

In the psychology of money, emotions are also quite important. Stress, worry, and terror related to money can influence our choices, causing us to make rash decisions, take unwarranted risks, or put off paying bills.Individuals can make better financial decisions by recognizing and resolving underlying biases, emotions, and beliefs by studying the psychology of money. Better financial practices like budgeting, saving, and intelligent investment can also be aided by this.

Therefore,understanding the intricate ways in which our beliefs, feelings, and prior financial experiences shape our attitudes and actions is made possible by studying the psychology of money. Investigating this area can result in a deeper self-awareness and, eventually, a more stable and satisfying financial existence.The influence of behavioral economics on one's financial security. The study of behavioral economics integrates ideas from economics and psychology to better understand how people make financial decisions. It investigates the cognitive biases, social influences, and emotional variables that shape people's financial decision-making. The realization that people frequently make irrational decisions is one of behavioral economics' main effects on financial well-being. Conventional economic theories operate under the premise that people are completely rational agents who always seek to maximize their own utility. Behavioral economics, however, emphasizes that people frequently make decisions that are not in their best interests because they are biased.

For instance, people may display a trait known as "loss aversion," in which they are more likely to experience the anguish of losses than the joy of victories. People may make illogical financial decisions as a result of this bias, such as selling winning investments too soon or holding onto losing ones for too long.In the field of behavioral economics, "present bias" or "hyperbolic discounting" is another important idea. The inclination for people to put short-term satisfaction ahead of long-term financial objectives is discussed here. For example, instead of saving or investing for their future financial security, people can prefer to have instant gratification by spending money on frivolous goods.Realizing these behavioral biases has led financial organizations and policymakers to create techniques and interventions that encourage people to make better financial decisions. Retirement savings rates have been seen to rise in response to strategies such as automatic enrollment in retirement savings schemes and default investment alternatives. Similarly, people can overcome cognitive biases and make better decisions if they are given clear and visually appealing information about the possible outcomes of financial actions.Furthermore, behavioral economics has shown the significance of social factors on financial judgment. Individuals frequently base their financial decisions on peer comparisons and social standards. This knowledge has been applied to projects such as social proof messaging, which tells people about how others with comparable circumstances have successfully obtained favorable financial results. Policymakers and organizations can promote beneficial financial behaviors and enhance overall financial well-being by utilizing social factors.

Money-related Attitudes And Ideas

An individual's money well-being is greatly influenced by their money thinking and ideas. Our understanding of how our beliefs, attitudes, and biases affect our financial decisions and behaviors is aided by the field of behavioral economics, which blends economics with psychology.

Beliefs about money are one facet of the money mindset. These ideas, which might be conscious or unconscious, have a big impact on the decisions we make about money. People who have a scarcity mindset, for instance, may hoard or exercise excessive caution while making purchases if they feel that money is hard to come by or rare. On the other hand, if someone thinks that wealth is plentiful and may be a useful instrument for influence and personal development, they might embrace a mindset of abundance, which can promote investing, risk-taking, and philanthropy.

Behavioral economists have discovered that our ability to make sound financial decisions is impacted by cognitive biases including present bias and loss aversion. Our inclination to fear losses more than we appreciate comparable gains is known as loss aversion. This bias may cause people to make illogical decisions, such as hanging onto lost investments out of a fear of losing money. Present bias is the tendency for us to put short-term objectives ahead of long-term objectives. It may show up as excessive spending, disregarding savings, or putting off crucial financial responsibilities like retirement planning.

Recognizing these biases aids in the creation of programs that encourage wiser financial decisions. For example, by presenting investing losses as opportunities for learning instead of failures, people might be more inclined to make strategic portfolio adjustments. Similar to this, implementing systems like automatic savings programs or linking long-term savings objectives to instant rewards can support responsible financial behavior and help counteract current bias.

Emotions' influence on financial decisions

The study of behavioral economics integrates concepts from economics and psychology to comprehend and explain how people make decisions. The awareness of the influence of emotions on financial decisions and overall financial well-being is a fundamental feature of behavioral economics.

Conventional economic models presuppose that people are logical and base their decisions on impartial evaluations of the costs, rewards, and probabilities. But behavioral economics acknowledges that emotions play a big role in our financial decisions, frequently causing us to stray from strictly rational conclusions.

Emotions that affect financial decision-making include fear, greed, overconfidence, and regret. For instance, during market downturns, fear of losing money might make people avoid taking essential risks or force them to sell investments before they should. Similar to this, greed might lead people to make snap decisions about their investments that don't fully weigh the hazards.

Furthermore, overconfidence can result in people overestimating their financial acumen and taking unwarranted risks, both of which can have negative effects. The regret feeling can lead people to make illogical financial decisions, such hanging onto failed investments for longer than required in order to escape the regret that comes with admitting defeat.

Achieving financial well-being requires an understanding of how emotions influence financial decisions. People who are aware of and control these emotional biases can make more unbiased and logical decisions about their spending, investing, and saving. This could entail strategies like establishing attainable financial objectives, exercising self-control and discipline, looking for a variety of financial advice sources, and becoming conscious of biases and emotional triggers.

Moreover, behavioral economics has impacted the financial services sector by encouraging the creation of goods and services that take consumers' emotional inclinations into account. When it comes to retirement savings programs, for example, the introduction of automatic enrollment and default contribution rates helps combat people's propensity to put off or be unduly careful with their investments.

<u>Techniques for altering your financial perspective</u>

Improving your financial well-being requires first changing your perspective about money. The following techniques will assist you in changing your viewpoint and creating a more positive connection with money:

1. **Identify and confront your limiting beliefs**: Begin by determining the

unfavorable assumptions or attitudes you hold toward money. These may have come from your childhood or been shaped by the messages that society sends out. Contest these ideas by raising doubts about their veracity and taking into account stronger, more empowering viewpoints.

2. **Develop a positive outlook on money:** By emphasizing plenty over scarcity. Recognize and be grateful for what you already have rather than focusing on what you lack. Develop an optimistic outlook for your financial future and cultivate thankfulness for the resources you already have.

3. **Establish specific financial goals**: To provide oneself with direction and a feeling of purpose, clearly define your financial goals. Divide them into more manageable, measurable goals that can be monitored. Setting goals will help you stay motivated and prioritize your financial choices.

4. **Become knowledgeable about personal finance**: Read books, go to workshops, or enroll in classes to expand your financial literacy. Recognize fundamental ideas such as debt management, investing, saving, and budgeting. Your level of confidence and

empowerment in managing your finances will increase with increased knowledge.

5. **Surround yourself with positive influences**: Get in the company of people who have a sound financial philosophy. Participate in discussions concerning personal money, consult professionals for guidance, and become a part of communities or support groups that concentrate on financial health. This nurturing atmosphere will foster your personal development and strengthen wise financial practices.

6. **Engage in mindful spending**: Pay attention to your spending patterns and make deliberate decisions. Consider

whether an item is in line with your financial objectives and values before making a purchase. Make a distinction between necessities and wants, then allocate your funds appropriately. To prevent excessive consumerism and impulsive purchases, cultivate self-discipline.

7. **Invest sensibly and save**: Begin saving on a regular basis, even if it's just a little sum. Create an emergency fund to guard against unforeseen costs. Investigate investment options gradually in line with your financial objectives and risk tolerance. Long-term financial security depends on investing and saving.

8. **Monitor your progress**: Keep an eye on things by reviewing your financial status on a regular basis. Maintain a record of your earnings, outlays, saves, and investments. By engaging in this routine, you may pinpoint areas for growth, maintain accountability, and modify your financial plans as needed.

Remind yourself that it takes time and effort to change your financial outlook. Have patience with yourself and acknowledge your little accomplishments as you go. You may improve your financial situation and build a more affluent future if you put in the necessary effort and adopt the appropriate mindset.

Chapter four

Creating a Well-Being Lifestyle

In terms of overall welfare, mindfulness has a lot to offer. It means avoiding judgment and purposefully concentrating attention on the present moment. Focusing on the present moment in order to reduce stress, increase self-awareness, and promote calm and clarity is known as mindfulness.

There are several ways that practicing mindfulness could enhance health. It can help people become more mentally and emotionally tough overall, improve their ability to focus and pay attention, and control their emotions and stress reactions. By engaging in mindfulness practices, people can become more conscious of their thoughts, feelings, and physical sensations as well as of themselves.

Mindfulness practice can also lead to positive changes in relationships and interpersonal interactions. Active listening and being fully present with others are two ways that people can improve their interpersonal connections and communicate more successfully.

Furthermore, mindfulness can improve physical well-being by reducing stress symptoms and improving sleep quality.

There are several health benefits associated with it, including reduced blood pressure, boosted immunity, and improved digestion. All things considered, incorporating mindfulness into your daily routine can improve your overall sense of wellness by promoting self-care, growing in self-awareness and compassion, and strengthening your connection to the present moment. Being content and feeling thankful are essential elements of overall wellness. They can improve our sense of happiness and fulfillment and help us develop a positive outlook on life. Well-being is enhanced by gratitude and contentment in the following ways:

1. **Perspective shift:** Expressing gratitude enables us to shift our emphasis from the things in our lives that are lacking to all of the blessings and plenty we already have. It makes it possible for us to enjoy life's small joys.

2. **Increased positivist**: Gratitude and contentment practices support a positive mindset. In spite of challenges or setbacks, it helps us to appreciate and be content in the present moment.

3. **Improved mental health**: Research suggests that being thankful reduces anxiety and symptoms of depression. It promotes happiness, lowers stress, and improves general mental health.

4. **Stronger bonds and improved relationships**: Relationships benefit from reciprocating gratitude. It helps us to appreciate and acknowledge the help and contributions of those who live close to us.

5. **Greater resilience**: By cultivating gratitude and satisfaction, we can strengthen our resilience to adversity. We can summon the strength to face challenges head-on by focusing on the positive aspects of our lives.

6. **Greater self-esteem**: When we are thankful and content, we divert our attention from making comparisons and chasing after other people's praise. They increase our sense of self-worth and

self-acceptance by assisting us in valuing and recognizing our unique qualities, accomplishments, and abilities.

Simple strategies for bringing thankfulness and contentment into our daily lives include keeping a gratitude journal, actively showing others how much we appreciate them, and taking a moment to acknowledge our benefits. By cultivating these disciplines, we can live more fulfilling lives and experience more well-being.

The relationship between good financial standing and physical well-being

The relationship between one's physical and financial well-being is nuanced and multifaceted. They may seem like different aspects of our lives, yet they are actually able to influence and affect each other in a variety of ways.

1. **Health-related costs**: Physical health problems can result in high medical costs, which can put a strain on one's finances. Costly medical procedures, prescription

drugs, and continuing care may result in debt or financial strain.

2. **Productivity and income**: Our capacity to work and earn a living is greatly influenced by our physical health. Physical restrictions or chronic illnesses can have an impact on our ability to perform well at work and grow professionally, which could lower our earning potential.

3. **Costs associated with insurance**: Whether it's health insurance or another kind of coverage, poor physical health can lead to higher insurance premiums. A history of health problems or per-existing diseases may raise premium costs or even result in coverage denial.

4. **Lifestyle decisions and costs**: Adopting a sedentary lifestyle, eating poorly, abusing drugs, or engaging in other physical health-related behaviors can all have an adverse effect on well-being in addition to raising costs. Financial hardships can result from medical procedures, frequent doctor visits, and unhealthy coping techniques.

5. **Mental health and decision-making**: Stress, anxiety, and sadness can be brought on by physical health problems that also affect our mental health. Decision-making processes, especially financial decisions, may be impacted by certain mental health issues. Financially speaking, making rash

or illogical judgments when it comes to investing or spending might have long-term effects.

It's critical to understand that there is no set relationship between financial and physical wellness. Proactive efforts to address both physical and financial wellness can lead to favorable outcomes, even while poor physical health might cause financial challenges. Potential financial obligations can be lessened by maintaining physical health through preventative measures, frequent exercise, a balanced diet, and receiving the necessary medical attention. Comparably, safeguarding one's physical well-being can be aided by concentrating on one's financial health through prudent spending, saving, debt management, and adequate insurance coverage. Pursuing a holistic approach to well-being that takes into account one's financial situation as well as physical health is essential for long-term stability and general quality of life.

Financial stability and sustainable livelihood

There are various ways in which sustainable living and financial security can coexist:

1. **Energy savings**: Adopting sustainable habits can assist lower energy expenses

over time and result in long-term financial benefits. Examples of these practices include adopting energy-efficient appliances, insulating dwellings, and utilizing renewable energy sources like solar power.

2. **Lessened consumption**: Living a sustainable lifestyle frequently entails cutting back on consumption and emphasizing quality over quantity. People can lower their expenses and free up more money for investing or saving by cutting back on frivolous spending and concentrating on necessities.

3. **Mode of transportation**: Choosing environmentally friendly modes of

transportation, such as riding a bike, carpooling, or taking public transit, not only lowers carbon emissions but also saves money on gas and auto maintenance.

4. **Waste reduction**: Cutting back on single-use items and adopting sustainable habits like composting and recycling can save money. People can avoid buying things they don't need and make better use of their resources by reducing waste.

5. **Health benefits**: Eating whole foods, exercising, and spending more time outside are all healthy behaviors that are frequently encouraged by sustainable living. By improving physical health,

these lifestyle choices may ultimately result in lower healthcare costs.

6. **Long-term financial resilience**: Adopting sustainable habits can help people align their investments with their principles and put them in a position to possibly profit financially from new trends and possibilities. Examples of these practices include investing in Eco-conscious businesses or renewable energy sources.

It's crucial to remember that, even while adopting Eco-friendly habits can improve financial well-being, there might be upfront fees involved. On the other hand, a lot of these investments have the potential to pay off in the long run and build a more stable and sustainable future.

Investing for the future Making

Prudent financial decisions such as investing for the future can pay off in the long run and contribute to your financial stability. Depending on your time horizon, risk tolerance, and financial objectives, there are a number of options to think about when it comes to investing. The following are important things to remember:

1. **Identify your financial objectives**: Establish your goals for the investments you make. Are you putting money aside

for your child's education, your own retirement, or a down payment on a home? Your investment approach will be guided more easily if you set clear targets.

2. **Recognize your risk tolerance**: Prior to making any investments, it's critical to determine your own level of risk tolerance. Although there is a chance for bigger returns with higher-risk investments, there is also a greater chance of volatility. Think about how comfortable you are with market swings.

3. **Diversify your portfolio**: Distributing your investments throughout several asset classes, industries, and geographical areas is a risk management technique known as

diversification. You might potentially minimize losses and lessen the effect of any one investment on your entire portfolio by diversifying.

4. **Take into account the time horizon**: The amount of time you intend to invest your money before you need it is known as your investment time horizon. A longer time horizon gives you more time to recover from market downturns, which permits you to take a more aggressive approach to investing.

5. **Investigate your investment alternatives**: Stocks, bonds, mutual funds, exchange-traded funds (ETFs), real estate, and more are just a few of the options for

investing that are out there. Spend some time learning about each option's past performance, related risks, and anticipated potential returns.

6. **Seek expert guidance**: Speaking with a financial advisor can be helpful if you are unsure or have no prior investment experience. They can assist in evaluating your financial status, designing an investing strategy that meets your objectives, and offering continuous direction and assistance.

7. **Keep an eye on and tweak your investments:** Make sure your portfolio is consistently in line with your objectives and risk tolerance. Over time, changes in

the economy, the market, and your personal situation may necessitate modifying your investing plan.

8. **Remain disciplined**: Investing is a long-term commitment, so it's critical to maintain discipline and refrain from making rash decisions based on transient market swings. Remain true to your financial strategy and refrain from making hasty decisions.

Keep in mind that there are dangers associated with investing and that profits are not always guaranteed. However, you can greatly improve your chances of creating a secure future with a carefully designed investing strategy that is founded on careful analysis and consideration of your financial objectives.

Chapter five

<u>Reinterpreting Contentment and Achievement</u>

Redefining financial well-being on a continuing basis reflects our growing awareness of what it really means to be successful and content in today's society. It explores a more holistic viewpoint that includes both financial security and emotional well-being, going beyond the conventional paradigm of only collecting riches and material belongings.

Realizing the value of financial education and literacy is one part of reframing financial well-being. We can help people traverse the complicated world of personal finance by providing them with the information and abilities to make wise financial decisions. This entails being aware of ideas like debt management, investing, saving, and budgeting.

Recognizing the importance of psychological and emotional aspects in our relationship with money is another step in the ongoing process of redefining financial well-being. To take a better and more balanced approach, we must address our attitudes, beliefs, and behaviors toward money. This could entail looking at our spending patterns, figuring out our values and financial objectives, and developing an abundance-based mindset as opposed to a scarcity-based one.

Moreover, there is a strong correlation between the notion of financial well-being and wider societal factors. It requires acknowledging the structural obstacles and disparities that keep some people and communities from taking use of financial opportunities and resources. In order to genuinely redefine financial well-being, we need to focus on building a more equal and inclusive financial system that enables prosperity for all.

Redefining financial well-being is ultimately a continuous process that requires introspection, education, and change. We must always seek to deepen and broaden our comprehension of what it means to have a happy and prosperous life. We can develop a society in which financial well-being is available to everyone by accepting this process and striving for a more thorough and inclusive approach.

Reassessing society's convection

Reassessing social norms is a crucial and continuous activity that enables us to scrutinize the expectations, values, and beliefs that influence our conduct as a group. By challenging established conventions, we can investigate alternate viewpoints and question long-held beliefs, which can ultimately result in constructive society transformation. Among other societal issues that may need to be reevaluated include consumerism, cultural norms, traditional gender roles, and the effects of the environment. We can promote a more diverse, equitable, and sustainable society that better fits our changing needs and ideals by critically thinking and having open discussions.

Discovering meaning and contentment

Discovering meaning and contentment is an incredibly personal path that differs for every person. Nonetheless, the following broad approaches can be useful in this investigation:

1. **Consider your values**: Begin by determining what is most important to you. Think about your guiding principles, your passions, and your essential values when making decisions. By giving these things some thought, you may make sense of your own values and provide the groundwork for discovering your purpose.

2. **Investigate your interests**: Take part in pursuits and pastimes that actually fascinate and thrill you. You might find new hobbies and passions that fulfill you by experimenting and pursuing your curiosity.

3. **Establish meaningful objectives**: Make sure your objectives reflect your values and aspirations. These objectives might be short- or long-term, and they can include a range of topics in your life, including your relationships, job, personal development, and community service. Having specific goals to strive for can give one a feeling of purpose and direction.

4. **Look for opportunities to contribute**: Seek out methods to improve your neighborhood or the wider community. This can be helping others, contributing to causes that are important to you, or finding employment that enables you to have a significant impact. Making a difference and helping others can deeply fulfill one's soul.

5. **Adopt a growth-oriented mindset**: Encourage an attitude of lifelong learning and personal advancement. This can entail pushing yourself, looking for new experiences, and having an open mind to development and change. Personal growth can broaden your horizons, help you

understand yourself better, and strengthen your sense of purpose in life.

6. **Develop thankfulness**: Show thanks by consistently recognizing and valuing the advantages and good things in your life. By practicing gratitude, you can change your perspective from what you lack to what you have, which will increase your sense of satisfaction and pleasure.

Discovering meaning and fulfillment is a continuous process that changes as you mature and develop. It's acceptable to take detours and seize fresh chances as you go. Have faith in yourself, remain receptive to learning, and let your path take its natural course.The point where happiness and financial success meet, The relationship between happiness and financial success is a complicated and multidimensional subject. A person's sense of security, independence, and capacity to satisfy their needs and ambitions can all be obtained through financial success, but happiness is not a given. Studies indicate that there is less of a relationship between income and happiness after fundamental necessities are satisfied.

A feeling of purpose, overall life satisfaction, meaningful connections, and general well-being are just a few of the many components that make up happiness. It's critical to understand that if other facets of life are neglected, even financial success on its own might not result in long-lasting satisfaction.

On the other hand, having enough money can make you happier by lowering stress, offering chances for personal development, fostering good memories, and improving general well being. It can provide people the flexibility to follow their hobbies, spend money on experiences, and foster deep connections.

In the end, each person's experience of the relationship between wealth and happiness is unique and subjective. It's critical to establish a healthy balance by giving other facets of life that enhance general happiness and well-being equal weight with the quest of financial success. This could entail developing deep connections, discovering a sense of direction in life, looking after one's physical and mental well-being, and pursuing fulfillment in a variety of spheres.

Individual testimonies of people who redefined their financial security

Numerous first-hand accounts exist of people who have redefined their financial security. Here are few instances:

1. Sarah quit her corporate job and launched her own small business. She initially struggled with money as she tried to launch her company. But as time went on, her business endeavors paid off, surpassing her prior earnings and giving her a stable salary and rewarding profession.

2. John and Lisa decided to adopt a more minimalist and reduced lifestyle. They downsized, sold their big home, gave away stuff they didn't need, and concentrated on leading a simpler, more purposeful life. Thanks to this adjustment, they were able to cut costs dramatically,

pay off debt, and devote more funds to things that made them happy and fulfilled.

3. Maria decided to shift careers in her 40's since she was dissatisfied with her corporate employment. She moved into a more fulfilling but lower-paying profession that matched her moral principles. Despite having less money, she felt more fulfilled and had a greater sense of purpose in life, therefore it was worth it.

4. Mark made the decision to become financially independent by using strict spending controls and proactive saving techniques. He lived below his means, made prudent investments, and carefully saved a sizable percentage of his salary.

He was able to retire early and follow his passions without worrying about money after a few years of focused saving.

These first-hand accounts demonstrate that attaining financial well-being involves more than just building wealth or a high income. It frequently entails making deliberate judgments, reassessing priorities, and coordinating financial choices with one's objectives and ideals. Every person's journey is different and is influenced by their goals, values, and environment.

<u>Conclusion</u>

An individual's subjective definition of financial well-being varies from person to person. It's more important to feel content, safe, and in charge of one's financial situation than it is to be wealthy or have a high income. A mix of financial preparation, knowledge, self-control, and awareness of one's financial options are frequently necessary to achieve financial well-being. One cannot stress the significance of having sound financial standing. It affects all facets of our existence, from relationships and future security to our own well-being. Making financial well-being a priority helps people build a better, wealthier future.

Financial well-being has undergone a radical transformation thanks to behavioral economics. Policymakers and organizations can create interventions and strategies that support people in making better financial decisions by identifying and taking into consideration cognitive biases, social effects, and emotional issues.Knowing behavioral economics can enable people to make decisions about their money that will lead to long-term stability and prosperity. It clarifies how our financial views and mindset affect our financial security. We may make better judgments, create healthier financial habits, and eventually attain more financial stability and prosperity by being aware of and taking action against cognitive biases.

In order for people to successfully navigate the complexity of personal money, financial literacy and education are necessary tools. People may take charge of their financial future and make educated decisions if they have the necessary information and abilities.

Investing entails risk, and diversity does not provide loss prevention or profit guarantees. It's critical to carry out in-depth research, keep up with market developments, and base judgments on your personal risk tolerance and financial status.

It's crucial to remember that there is risk involved with any investment. Examine your financial objectives, risk tolerance, and personal circumstances thoroughly before making any investing decisions. To assist you manage the dangers and complexities of investing, you should also think about consulting with a licensed financial advisor.

I urge and strongly advise readers to go out on a path to redefine financial well-being. Many people want to be financially stable and prosperous, and starting the journey in that direction is crucial. Here are some important things to think about:

1. Examine your income, expenses, obligations, and assets in detail to get a sense of your present financial status. This evaluation will provide you a comprehensive view of your financial situation and assist you in identifying areas that need care.

2. Establish attainable objectives: Specify your immediate and long-term financial objectives. Having clear goals may give you direction and inspiration for any

financial endeavor, be it retirement savings, debt repayment, or emergency fund building.

3. Make a budget: Create a budget that is reasonable and in line with your financial objectives. Maintain a record of your earnings and outlays, rank the costs that are most important, and pinpoint areas where you may reduce wasteful spending. You can make sure you reach your financial objectives and efficiently manage your resources by creating a well-thought-out budget.

4. Educate yourself: Invest some time in learning about personal finance concepts and broadening your financial horizons.

Your ability to make wise decisions that improve your financial well-being will increase as you gain more knowledge about investing, money management, and other financial topics.

5. Seek expert assistance: Take into consideration speaking with a planner or financial advisor who can provide tailored counsel depending on your unique situation. They may offer insightful information on a variety of topics, including tax planning, retirement planning, and investment possibilities. They can also assist you in developing a customized financial strategy that supports your objectives.

6. Develop sound financial practices: Save money systematically, make prudent purchases, and stay out of debt. Review your financial status on a regular basis, look for ways to improve, and make changes as needed. Long-term financial well-being is mostly built via resilience and consistency.

7. Adopt a growth mindset: A mentality change is necessary to redefine financial well-being. Adopt a constructive mindset regarding finances, perceive obstacles as chances for personal development, and keep your eyes on the prize of long-term financial achievement. Developing a

development mentality enables you to get past obstacles, adjust to changes, and carry on with your financial journey.

Redefining financial well-being is a continuous process that reflects our changing perception of what it means to be successful and secure in today's fast-paced world. In the past, a person's capacity to meet basic requirements and build riches was frequently the only indicator of their financial well-being. But now, a broader notion of financial health is included in this definition.

These days, a comprehensive approach is taken to financial well-being, accounting for a number of variables including income, spending, managing debt, saving, investing, and general financial literacy. It acknowledges that having a particular quantity of money is not the only factor in determining financial stability; knowledge and expertise in making wise financial decisions and navigating intricate financial systems are equally important.

Moreover, the reinterpretation of financial well-being recognizes the significance of personal values, objectives, and ambitions. It acknowledges that each person's financial journey is distinct and that what one person may consider to be financially healthy may not be the same for another. It highlights the necessity of individualized approaches to financial planning and exhorts people to match their financial choices with their long-term goals and core values.

Understanding the relationship between finances and general well-being is another essential component in redefining financial well-being. It recognizes the close relationship between financial health and other aspects including relationships, emotional and physical well-being, and a feeling of purpose. Finding a balance that enables one to live a meaningful and sustainable life is more important for achieving financial well-being than giving up one's general well-being.

Furthermore, the dynamic character of re framing financial well-being is a result of both society and economic shifts. A new outlook on financial well-being is required due to factors including automation, globalization, employment market shifts, and technology improvements. It necessitates adjusting to new financial opportunities and obstacles, such the gig economy, the emergence of digital currencies, and shifting retirement landscapes.

To sum up, the continuous process of redefining financial well-being is indicative of a wider realization that financial health is dynamic and cannot be characterized by a uniform strategy. It entails taking into account a variety of factors, matching financial decisions to one's ideals, and acknowledging that the economic environment is constantly changing. We can better prepare people to achieve long-term financial security and general well-being by regularly reviewing and revising our knowledge of financial well-being.

www.ingramcontent.com/pod-product-compliance
Lightning Source LLC
Chambersburg PA
CBHW070856260726
48661CB00004B/1434